How to
Pull Women

How to Pull Women
Everything You Need to Know

Clive "Rock Solid" Webb

CARLTON
BOOKS

First published 2004 by

Carlton Books Limited
20 Mortimer Street
London W1T 3JW

ISBN 1 84442 784 6

Typeset by e-type, Liverpool

Printed and bound in Great Britain

10 9 8 7 6 5 4 3 2 1

DEDICATION

To mum & dad, and all the women
I have ever had the pleasure of.

Contents

Introduction

From geek to god – transform yourself.

Have you ever found yourself sitting down and thinking that no matter how hard you seem to try, you just can't pull a woman?

When you speak to an attractive woman, do your palms sweat, does your mouth go dry and your speech resemble the after effects of a mouth full of helium? Do you walk up to someone only to find that you don't know what to say, or simply put your foot right in it straight away? Or do you not even have the courage to approach someone in the first place?

If any of these descriptions fits you then let me reassure you that you are definitely not alone. There are literally thousands of guys out there, all in the same boat as you, all looking for fun of the female variety and all of them ending up alone at the end of the evening.

That is why I wrote this book. I too was like you once and, believe it or not, probably even worse. So, here in my own words is a little bit about my life and how I managed to transform myself from a failure with women into the silver-tongued charmer I am today.

I started wearing glasses when I reached the age of 11. Big, thick 'Joe 90' ones. You know the sort – the ones guaranteed to attract the attention of the school bully, fists flailing and feet flying, but not the girls (unless you count being called 'speccy' or 'four eyes' as a sign of females being attracted to you). And after all, the girls were the ones I really wanted to impress.

To add further insult to injury, I was thin as well. As if wearing television screens on my face didn't make it bad enough, I actually made the school javelin look obese!

So you can see, then, why my teen years were not destined to be spent whiling away the hours with local girls on lovers' lane. Instead, my days and nights were spent staring by torchlight at my elder brother's well-thumbed copies of *Mayfair* and *Playboy*, which were hidden under his pile of neatly folded jumpers.

Like all kids my age, I sat goggled-eyed (and let me tell you, with my glasses that bit was easy) and in awe at pictures of a beefy bloke called Charles Atlas who used to stare back all muscles and leopardskin loincloth from the pages of a yellowing *News of the World*.

His adverts promised anyone who could scrape together the wherewithal the chance to swap not only their skinny frame for a body festooned with muscles but – more importantly to me – the promise of success with girls!

Unfortunately, my meagre pocket money didn't stretch far enough to cover the cost of his bodybuilding course. But one day, during a long summer holiday from school, I happened to stumble upon my dad's old weightlifting set, rusting and dirty, forgotten and neglected in the furthest corner of the garden shed and started to train.

It was hard going, as I had no knowledge except for a beginner's guide to weightlifting loaned from the local library. But as time progressed, I soon discovered that this was to be my golden fleece, the pathway to success, and boy was I going to use it.

I trained like a man – sorry, boy – possessed. Over the next few years my muscles grew rapidly – but unfortunately, my confidence didn't keep pace. I still looked like Joe 90 and, although the other boys started to admire and even fear me because of my growing, Popeye-like build, I found I still hadn't got the confidence to speak to girls, let alone chat them up.

So it went on, until a few years later, I met the lady who was to change my life. Let me tell you what happened. I had been working in a variety of jobs for a while but still didn't have that much luck with women as, although now big and muscular, I still wore glasses – albeit trendy ones. I still lacked confidence and didn't have a clue how to approach women or what to say to them.

This was all to change when I started work in a large hotel in Stratford-upon-Avon as a hall porter. I enjoyed it immensely from the start, as I was meeting people – and I even had the odd relationship with female members of staff.

One day, while I was serving at one of the hotel's conference rooms between sessions, I met a lady who was totally different to everyone else I'd ever met, and she really interested me. She was lecturing at a company conference based in the hotel and I listened avidly as she talked about things that were alien to my ears. She spoke about body language, positive thinking and things called 'positive suggestion' and 'neuro-linguistic programming'. She explained how they could be used to help you get what you wanted and to make you feel good about yourself.

I was hooked and wanted to find out more, so, while helping her to load up her car, I plucked up the courage to ask her about the subject of her lecture. She replied that she had seen me watching and asked whether I was interested in learning more. Of course, I jumped at the chance and, to cut a long story short, over the course of the next six months she taught me skills and techniques that were to change my life forever.

Using these new-found skills my confidence soared. No more did I avoid busy pubs for fear of not being able to mix and speak to people. With my training I looked good and, coupled with her teachings, I felt better about myself and more confident than ever before.

Over the next few years my life really took off. Relationship followed relationship and I found myself not only meeting but also bedding loads of gorgeous women. And I can only put it down to my new-found self-confidence.

The new me started taking up different jobs, ones I never would have contemplated before. I worked as a barman, qualified as a fitness coach, worked in local health clubs and even did some modelling. All the time I was using and honing my new-found skills to approach, talk to and ultimately seduce beautiful women. It was fantastic! It seemed that I could have any woman who caught my eye – and I took full advantage of it, I can tell you.

My friends and fellow colleagues at the hotel were amazed at the transformation in me. New female members of staff or customers would arrive and the other guys would flock around them trying to impress.

Then, when they had tried and failed, yours truly would step in and seal the deal apparently without even trying. Many times the lady in question would totally ignore the others and make a beeline straight for me.

Life continued on this roller coaster until one day I saw an advert for budding male strippers in a national entertainment newspaper. I had heard all about these guys – half-men, half-horses whom women adored and who repaid the compliment by sleeping with them at the drop of a G-string. Needless to say, I too wanted to be in on the act.

I knew deep down that I could do it, so I dialled the number advertised. To cut another long story short, I auditioned and, four short weeks later, after tiring rehearsals, I was part of a five-man troupe working the length and breadth of the country entertaining (in more ways than one) sex-hungry women. A hard job I know, but someone had to do it.

Over the next ten years or so I had a ball and lost count of the number of women I slept with (although sleep was obviously the last thing on my mind). There were hundreds, ranging from professional types to housewives and students – in fact, all sorts. And all of them taught me something about what it was that women wanted and what men needed to do to get it.

Sometimes we would even sit and talk (I know, it's hard to believe but it's true) and they would tell me about their boring lives and how the only reason their toes curled up during sex with their husbands was because they couldn't be bothered to take their tights off!

I worked with other strippers, both male and female, met male escorts and porn actors, all the time gathering information and using it in my quest to be the best.

Friends were jealous of my success with women, so I decided to help them by revealing some of my secrets. In turn, armed with their increased knowledge and skills, they too increased their self-confidence, turned their previous bad luck with women around completely and started winning.

So why, I hear you ask, after a lifetime of women throwing themselves at your feet, are you divulging all for others to share? Well, I'll be honest. Apart from the money I'm set to make from the sale of this book, I have two other reasons for writing it.

The first is that I have finally met the woman of my dreams. She is gorgeous, 25 years old and I have vowed from this day to be faithful. Secondly, I was just like you were and know exactly how you feel each time you get knocked back by a woman or let the opportunity to speak to her pass you by because of your shyness and lack of confidence. I want to help, and what better way than by telling you how I did it myself?

I don't need this information any more myself and may as well share it with others who do and who are in the same boat as I was. Chances are that some of the things I'm going to tell you you'll already know, but most will be new to you. It's best to start at the beginning and not be tempted to go straight to the 'On the pull' chapter – I know it's important and has its place, but remember, you have to learn to walk before learning to run. Unless, that is, there's an irate husband bearing down on you with a 12-bore in his hand, in which case I suggest you run like hell!

Adapt and personalize the information given to suit yourself and the situation you find yourself in. Give it a chance and I'm sure you'll be amazed by the results. You don't need loads of money, a fast car, big house or expensive clothes to succeed with women – after all, you can't take that little lot to bed with you and your conquest, now can you? Neither do you need to be square-jawed and handsome. One of my friends who uses the very techniques I'll be telling you about manages to pull loads of women, and he's 25 stone with more chins than a WeightWatchers session in Texas!

So, be positive, read, learn and put into practice. You

have nothing to fear except fear itself. One very important thing to remember is if you always do what you always did you'll always get what you always got. This guide will work, I guarantee it. I just wish it had been around when I was Joe 90 – it would have saved me so much time.

Chapter One | **Self-confidence**

Gain sizzling self-confidence and jaw-dropping self-esteem

Today is YOUR day.

As I mentioned earlier, before you go steaming in to the 'On the Pull' part of this book, searching for what you think are tried-and-tested chat-up lines, I want you firstly to concentrate on this chapter for a while. After all, I'm sure you'll agree that there's no point going out to attract women armed with all the chat-up lines under the sun if you haven't actually got the guts to use them, now is there?

As a practical example, I'm going to tell you the story of how I discovered self-confidence for myself to prove that what I'm going to tell you is fact not fiction and has worked for someone else.

My story starts when I was working as a fitness instructor in a gym in Stratford-upon-Avon in the early 1990s. I was having what I thought then was a successful time seducing female clients and honing my pulling skills to perfection, when I happened to meet the actor Charles Dance.

I remember it like it was yesterday. The gym was full, as usual, with actors who were appearing at the local theatre and training in the gym, when Charles Dance walked into reception and enquired about membership – although I really should say 'glided' instead of 'walked', as he seemed to float in on a cushion of air. Without exception, everyone in the place just stood and stared at this vision of a man, their mouths open wider than Arnold Schwarzenegger's shoulders.

As he stood and chatted he seemed to radiate some kind of aura around him, some special quality that made people take notice and set him aside from everyone else in the room, and this intrigued me. It was some time later that I was to find out exactly what this quality was. I discovered that it goes by the name of 'self-confidence'.

There are other people out there who have self-confidence, just like Charles Dance, and it's possible for you to achieve it too. In this chapter I am going to teach you how to become so hot that any woman within a five-mile radius is going to have to pack asbestos gloves in her handbag before she even gets to meet you – and that's a fact!

The very first step to gaining self-confidence is to believe in yourself. This sounds easy. We all know it's possible when things are going great for you. But when the bottom seems to be falling out of your world, it's a completely different story.

To make things easier, I first want to destroy one popular misconception that people have about self-confidence and that is that you have to have to be perfect in order to have it. This is absolute and utter rubbish. After all, what is perfect? All of us have bits we like about ourselves and bits we don't, and when all's said and done it's just one person's opinion against another as to what constitutes perfection.

So the most important opinion in gaining self-confidence for yourself is your own opinion and no one else's. It's yours that counts. When you get that bit right the other bits will soon follow and fall into place.

The next step to gaining self-confidence is to learn to understand one very important thing about yourself, and that is how other people actually see you. When you start thinking about this you can then progress to realizing that it's not what they think about you that matters, but what you think about yourself.

As a male stripper I stood on stage thousands of times in my career. Even though loads of women loved me up there, it was the way I felt about myself that really counted and that's what gave me the confidence to stand up on stage in the first place. The end result was that the audience loved me (and I was told that I did too).

One practical way to identify how you really see yourself is to examine things that you do in your everyday life. All of us, without exception, carry out positive acts during our lives, and we get rewarded in return. These acts may take place at work – for example, when the boss congratulates you on meeting a tight deadline. The reward may be simply a smile from someone in the street as you hold the door open so they can go through first. We never seem to remember these 'rewards', but funnily enough when we do something negative or someone says something bad about us, it's those actions that we seem to recall and dwell upon.

I have lost count of the number of compliments I received during my stripping career that went completely over my head. On one particular occasion, however, when some woman said that my ears were too big and my eyes too close together, I found myself listening hard and remembering her comment for a while afterwards before stepping out on stage again. (One thing did puzzle me, though: I was a male stripper, after all – shouldn't she have been concentrating on my other body parts instead?)

One practical way to discover how you see yourself is

by making a list. Take a pen and piece of paper and write down a list incorporating all of your talents and good qualities. Be honest and don't be shy when doing this – no one else is going to see it.

Your list could contain anything – for example, your beaming pearly white smile, your incredible talents on the old green baize, your smooth muscular chest, in fact anything you like. Go on, write them all down and when you're finished you may even surprise yourself and discover that you're happier about yourself than you ever imagined. I did this myself many years ago and that's how I managed to pluck up the courage to audition for the male strip troupe – and, thinking back, I'm so glad I did.

Once you've finished this list (hope you didn't have to leave the house to stock up on paper), I want you to write another list, but this time detailing all the things you enjoy doing. It could be going to see a film, watching the home team score that fantastic scorcher of a goal or sinking a few beers after a hard day at work – anything.

List the things you currently like doing and add others that you don't currently do but would like to, being as realistic and as honest as possible, as no matter how amazing the information I give you, some things are just plain impossible. While writing these lists you should start to see a pattern emerge that should tell you that you didn't actually realize how many good points you had and although you didn't recognize them yourself until now, others probably did.

These people are the ones who have been giving you the recognition you truly deserve and now's the time for you to start doing the same for yourself. You are a diamond. It's time to start shining.

Now I want you to write down another list, and this one should contain all the bad points you think you have. Be honest again, as we all have them. When you've finished (it'll be interesting to see which list was the longest), I want you to read it. Then rip it up.

'ARE YOU MAD?' I hear you ask. The answer to that question is 'No.' Go on, I want you to read it then rip it up and throw it away, as from this moment on you are going to concentrate only on the positive list you made earlier and put the negative one completely out of your mind.

Now, take hold of the good list you made earlier (sounds like *Blue Peter*, doesn't it?) and select any one of the positive things you wrote down that result in you feeling good about yourself. Concentrating on this one thing, I now want you to leg it down the nearest newsagents and get hold of some of those little round sticky coloured labels they sell in packets. When you've got them I want you to go around the house sticking them in places you come into contact with most during the day. This could be somewhere like the light switch in the bathroom, the fridge door, your wardrobe – anywhere, in fact.

These stickers you've just put up are from now on going to be referred to as your 'hot spots', and every time you see one you are going to touch it, at the same time remembering the positive attribute and action you chose earlier from your list. By doing this you will imprint upon your subconscious the fact that you do good things and more importantly that people really like you.

Another powerful way of reinforcing these beliefs is again to take the positive act chosen earlier and associate it with a simple action or gesture that you can perform whenever and wherever you are. It could be something like touching your nose, or perhaps your ear. Whichever you choose, each and every time you do it at the same time I want you to conjure up a mental picture of yourself carrying out the positive act. This will automatically have the effect of making you feel more confident and happy about yourself.

Carrying out this action is known as 'triggering' and as you continue to do it regularly you will soon find it'll become second nature. Then, just by carrying out your chosen trigger you will automatically feel more confident.

In practical terms, this technique can be used when you find yourself in a situation where you are feeling self-conscious or nervous. Due to the subtle nature of the trigger used, you can boost your self-confidence without anyone suspecting what you are up to.

Talking of self-confidence, I bet you didn't realize that one of the least-known but most important components of self-confidence is a thing called imagination. That swot of a kid at junior school with all those exciting stories about what he did during the school holidays had imagination galore and, although you probably hated him and made his life a misery by putting bricks in his sports bag and compasses in the back of his head, you must admit that he was probably the most confident kid in the class.

You too can use your imagination to make important changes, the ones that matter in your life and the ones you really want. The way to achieve this is by using a very powerful tool called 'Positive Suggestive Programming'.

Positive Suggestive Programming, or PSP as I will refer to it to from now on, uses the power of your mind to change things and actually make them happen. It is widely used in all walks of life – especially by athletes to psyche themselves up prior to important events.

One brilliant example I remember from my youth was

watching the film *Pumping Iron* with the great bodybuilder Arnold Schwarzenegger. He was competing in Pretoria, South Africa, for the Mr Olympia physique contest and the morning of the show found him telling the other competitors – including 'the Hulk', Lou Ferrigno – that he had called his mother the previous evening to tell her that he had won the contest. When Arnold's mother reminded him that the contest was not due to take place until the next day he replied that in his mind's eye he had already won it and it was to be. The other competitors' faces fell as he commiserated with them and, when contest time came, sure enough Arnold did indeed win. The technique Arnold used was the same as PSP and I'm sure you'll agree that he could never ever be described as lacking in self-confidence. He told himself that it was going to happen and it did. This is the power of PSP.

I myself have personally used the PSP techniques I'm going to describe to you to put me in the right frame of mind before a big strip show. I would sit and imagine myself standing on stage with the whole crowd of women on their feet cheering, screaming and applauding me. In my mind's eye each and every one of those women found me irresistible, so when the time actually came for me to walk on stage I already had them in the palm of my hand.

The way PSP works is by putting you in the right frame of mind so that when you set out to do something you actually succeed in carrying it out. Sprinters picture themselves crossing the finishing line first, weightlifters picture that world record weight held aloft, and they're all using techniques based on the principles of PSP.

PSP is one of the most powerful mind tools available to man to build self-confidence. By suggesting to yourself what you want to happen, several things are guaranteed:

- You will gain self-confidence.
- You will feel more positive about yourself and your abilities.
- Any negative thoughts you previously had about yourself will disappear.

The reason negative thoughts disappear is that you are actually focussing less on them and using more of your effort to focus on the things that you feel confident about and the things you really want. This was echoed when you destroyed the negative list you wrote earlier, by the hot spots you put up around your home and by the triggering used to remind yourself about the positive you. All of these techniques place negative thoughts to the back of your mind and elevate the positive ones to a higher plane.

PSP really is the easiest and quickest way to open new doors (sorry, but the one to J-Lo's dressing room is a bit more difficult – you may need a battering ram) and exciting opportunities.

You may think that PSP is a skill you have to learn to acquire (or just old-fashioned rubbish) but that's not so. The truth is you have actually had this ability yourself all the time but have never been able to recognize or use it.

Let me tell you, I was really amazed the first time I used it and I'm sure you'll feel the same way when you try it for yourself. The first step to using PSP is to decide what you really want to change about your life. It could be that new car, a fantastic physique to replace your wobbling belly or even attracting that great-looking girl you see every Friday in the local club – in fact, anything you want.

Write a list containing all of the changes you really want to make, and it's now time to start PSP for yourself. Take the list you've written and start imagining yourself actually having the things on it. Imagine yourself driving that flash motor, or showing off that chiselled torso on a crowded beach. As far as the girl from the club goes, do I really need to remind you what to imagine about her? I thought not.

The next step is to relax and just close your eyes – that's all. I know it sounds too easy to be of any real effect, but let me tell you that although simple, this next step is possibly the most important of all. Try and do it in as comfortable a place as possible, somewhere you won't be disturbed, though not somewhere you might find yourself falling asleep and certainly not at your work station – otherwise it'll be the boss doing the positive suggesting and you starting to look for another job, pronto!

So relax, close your eyes, breathe deeply and start to imagine all the things you want. When you're in this state your mind is in its most receptive state and you need to feed it the images one at a time till you've thought about everyone on your list.

While picturing the things you want, make sure you do it in such a realistic and positive way that you feel you already have them and are living them. You should picture the car's gleaming bodywork, feel the soft leather seats against your skin and hear the smooth purr of the engine as you roar along the open road. Feel those taut, smooth, rock-hard muscles growing daily in the gym, hear the women on the beach gasp and drool as you reveal that rippled torso and the squeal of delight from the girl in the club as you smoothly walk over and ask her to dance. It sounds so simple, but I can assure you it really will work.

Now that you've imagined these scenarios I'm going to ask you to do something that will totally convince you that I am, in fact, a complete and utter loony. What I want you to do is to give yourself permission to have whatever it is that's written on your list.

I know it sounds unbelievable, and even slightly mad, but it does work. I admit that I felt exactly the same way as you are now feeling when I first tried it, but I guarantee you won't be able to get what you really want without doing it first. Trust me.

Picture each image in turn and straight afterwards repeat to yourself, 'I give myself permission...' for whatever is on your list. Repeat this a couple of times and then move on to the next item. Repeat again for each item on the list and then affirm it as being a true statement of your desires.

Affirming further reinforces your permission to have what you desire. This affirmation goes by the form of a positive statement about yourself and your desires, such as, 'I WILL have that car, it WILL be mine'. This is a really powerful and important part of the whole PSP process and not just one to make you look a right 'nana.

Now you've done this it's time to look and act the part

of the role you're playing. Lengthy scientific studies show that what you look at and the things you experience affect the way you feel – it's obvious. Let's say you're a United fan and they're playing like dinner ladies in wellingtons – that's obviously going to make you feel angry and miserable. Similarly, watching Buffy slaying decaying, fang-toothed vampires while wearing tight jeans makes you feel a completely different man in all respects.

This is simply because when we see a happy, pleasant image our brains release certain hormones into the body. Studies reveal that these hormones act as the body's natural opiates, causing a pleasant 'high'.

In realistic terms, each time you see yourself as being confident and successful you again release a steady stream of these 'happy hormones' into your system, and this has the effect of making you feel even better about yourself.

Acting the part also helps confirm what you have promised yourself. When I auditioned to be a part of the strip troupe I dressed in the way I thought a stripper would dress and I can honestly say that I think it helped me get chosen. Actors very often research the character they are auditioning to play by wearing clothes and adopting mannerisms during their personal life to get into the part and give the casting director an exact picture of the character.

PSP uses all of these techniques and can help you to get anything you want and change your life around. The real beauty of these techniques is that you need nothing more than a comfortable place to sit or lie, peace and quiet and the most important thing: your imagination.

The best time to practise PSP is just before going off to sleep. Carrying out the techniques described at this time will help you relax more and drift off more quickly, as during sleep your subconscious can also concentrate solely on your desires. It's no coincidence that at some time or other we must all have had something on our minds just before retiring for the night and on waking have realized that we dreamt about the very same thing.

We are now at the end of this chapter. However barking mad you think I am after reading this, I guarantee these techniques have worked for me and countless others and will work for you in exactly the same way. I was transformed from looking like a lollipop wearing two cola bottles to one of the top 20 male strippers in the country, adored by thousands of women. I can honestly say that this amazing transition was all down to the techniques I've described. What are you waiting for? You have nothing to lose and everything to gain. So stop dreaming, start picturing and start scoring.

Chapter Two | **Sex appeal**

The ace down your trousers

If you're anything like I was all those years ago you probably feel as though women are attracted to you as much as a grizzly bear craves a nice veggie nut roast. You may also be convinced that you don't actually possess one iota of sex appeal, so I'm going to tell you something that's going to immediately destroy that myth. There are lots of people in the world who are considered stereotypically 'ugly' but who have loads of sex appeal and are, subsequently, a hit with the opposite sex (unlike you, who probably think the opposite sex just wants to hit you) – proving you don't always need an Adonis-like physique or handsome face to be considered attractive.

Now you know that, it's time to stop blaming yourself for all your past failures and meet the real you. Take me for example: I'm 41, my hair has been thinning for years (thank God for Grant from *EastEnders* making it fashionable) and I have worn glasses since the age of 11, yet I have slept with hundreds of women. So if I can do it then you certainly can.

OK then, if what I've said is true then what exactly is this sex appeal I keep banging on about and how do you get it? The answer is PSP, that's how. Yes that's right, specific techniques used in the previous chapter on self-confidence can be tailor-made for this very subject. After using these techniques I felt completely different about myself. And the great thing was that other people did too – especially women.

People such as Charles Dance have sex appeal, you can feel the aura around them the minute they enter the room, and it's this aura that makes them irresistible to the opposite sex. Women are intrigued by such men and want to get to know them better. And you too can be like them if you practise the techniques I'm going to describe.

Women will want to be seen with you, compete for your attention – and more! This 'secret' that up until now you didn't have is called 'charisma' and I'm going to show you exactly how to get it.

The following techniques are specifically designed to show you how to attain charisma and sex appeal. Try them for yourself with an open mind and I think you'll be amazed.

The first thing to do to gain sex appeal and charisma is, again, to relax somewhere quiet so you can fully concentrate on what it is I'm asking you to do. When you've done that I want you to close your eyes and picture yourself mentally. Look closely at yourself: are you standing tall with your shoulders back, stomach in and chest out? If not, then picture yourself slowly changing, growing to your full height, your head up and chin well forward.

Picture your shoulders getting broader and your whole appearance changing before your very eyes and then imagine yourself smiling. When we smile it automatically puts us in a happier frame of mind – and it also takes more muscles to frown than to smile, so it's physically easier too.

Now imagine yourself slipping on a tight white cotton vest and feel it as it hugs every contour of your torso. Look down to see the word 'STUD' start to appear in big black bold letters covering your chest. (Don't laugh, I'm absolutely serious.) The vest is skin-tight and the letters really stand out, impressing yourself and all who see it.

I now want you to imagine yourself leaving the house and walking down the local high street while wearing this vest (best put on your imaginary trousers as well, otherwise you'll be imagining yourself up in front of the local imaginary magistrates on an imaginary indecency charge!)

Picture yourself walking down the street while

wearing this vest. It's a bright sunny day and there are plenty of people about, especially gorgeous women. Everyone is smiling at you as you pass and some women are even crossing the road to get a closer look at you. You hear them complimenting you as they pass, saying, 'Who is that guy?, he's gorgeous' and 'Bet he's famous.'

Ask yourself how you feel now. I bet you're feeling more confident, happier and more attractive than you have ever felt before. I knew you would. By imagining yourself looking and feeling this way, you are able to alter the way you walk, feel and project your image. You can wear clothes that others wouldn't dare, and even wearing the same clothes as others will still have people looking at you in an admiring way and not them.

A friend of mine who lives in London has a habit of wearing a big black top hat perched on his head 24/7. It's absolutely enormous but it suits him because he has charisma. If anyone else wore it they would be a laughing stock, but he knows he looks good in it and the women flock round him. He is confident and it shows by his walk and the way he projects himself.

It's time to take this a stage further, so again imagine yourself wearing this vest but picture yourself this time in a club. It's late, noisy and the party's been in full swing for hours by the time you arrive. The place is packed with beautiful people and they're all having a good time. (I'm there, of course – can't you see me there in the back with those two gorgeous ladies?)

As you imagine yourself entering the room, I want you to stop for a second in the doorway and 'frame' yourself. It's a known fact that people's first impressions are the ones that count, so if you walk straight into the room, their gazes have to follow you and you have less chance of making your best impression.

By 'framing' yourself you are making a statement, just like a picture on a wall, that says, 'Stop, look at me.' Now imagine yourself standing like this as everyone's gaze turns to meet yours. Imagine the other guys in the room looking on enviously, but the women looking on adoringly, smiling and showing their appreciation.

Imagine yourself entering the main area of the club and looking around the room. Let your gaze fall on the most beautiful woman there – that's it, that's the one, the one all the guys are trying to impress. As you look over, imagine her ignoring the other guys and turning to look straight at you. Imagine her smiling, then watch as she stands and walks across the room toward you, all the time never letting her eyes leave yours.

Say 'Hi' and then take her arm and begin leading her out of the room, all the time noticing the other women present as they look on jealously and hear them say, 'That woman is so lucky, he is the best-looking guy here.'

Now affirm that this is what you want to happen by saying to yourself slowly over and over again, 'I am so hot, NO woman can resist me.'

Imagine this scenario enough times and I guarantee that when you put yourself into the actual situation it will happen. Picture this or other chosen positive scenarios each time before you leave the house, using this statement coupled with touching your 'hot spots'. You should also look in the mirror, smile and repeat to yourself 'I am Number One' then picture yourself as Number One just before stepping out of the door. You are the best and everyone knows it.

I mentioned in the previous chapter that an ideal time to practise PSP is before sleep and in the pursuit of sex appeal, here is an exercise that you can try to good effect.

Imagine writing the word 'stud' across your chest in bright red, bold lipstick, writing it in capital letters so that it stands out against your skin. Now close your eyes as you drift off, all the time imagining yourself dating loads of beautiful women. Imagine how it would really feel to do this, the smell of their skin and their touch. Now as you drift off, say to yourself over and over again, 'I am a stud, I can score with any woman I want.' You may well be surprised how you feel when you wake up.

This is easily one of the most powerful techniques for making things happen. The more you practise these techniques the more confident you'll feel and the more women will want to be around you. I went from being painfully shy and a loser with girls as a teenager to performing on stage in front of, and sleeping with, hundreds of women, so I am living proof that these techniques actually do work.

PSP coupled with positive affirmations are a very powerful combination. Use them both wisely and at the next club or party you go to, you won't just break the ice, you'll shatter it.

Chapter Three|**Grooming**

Soap and water

just won't wash

There are two things guaranteed to put women off men and they are:

- The man being more attractive than the woman.
- The man hogging the bathroom so much it stops her from getting herself in there for her daily three-hour shower.

The reason women feel like this is because vanity in a man equals insecurity and women can't stand it. Since time began they have yearned for a man strong and fearless like the ones described in the romantic novels you pick up and idly thumb through in the doctor's waiting room. (Because some wrinkly old granny has managed to get her wizened old hands on this month's copy of *Top Gear* and is noisily dribbling all over the article you particularly wanted to read on that beast of a car, the Mitsubishi Evolution.)

But don't panic, my eager beaver, and don't ditch those lotions and potions just yet, or throw away that aerosol and go 'au naturel'. Because in the next few pages I am going to reveal the best top-to-toe rules of men's grooming.

Follow them to the letter and see a marked change in your fornication fortune...

Hair

If you have any doubts as to how your crowning glory matches up, then the easiest thing to do is run your fingers through it, as this is what a woman will want to do during a passionate moment. And the first thing she'll want to see is: it is squeaky clean and flaky free? Fingernails encrusted with dirt or something with the consistency of soap powder will seriously hinder your chances of getting any further than 'just good friends'.

It doesn't matter whatever your choice of style or colour, as you can't beat a good scrub with a popular brand shampoo and conditioner. This will guarantee that your barnet is as hygienic and finger-friendly as your local restaurant after the environmental health officer has paid a visit.

Remember to get it cut regularly (after all, you can always try out your newly found confidence on that tasty girl in the unisex salon), though don't be too worried about keeping up with all the latest fashion trends. David B may change his hairstyle more frequently than Victoria's underwear, but as long as yours isn't a style that's too dated and it still suits you, there's not too much of a problem.

Should you be the sort, though, who drags your caveman-like bulk into the shower only to find more hair disappearing down the plug hole than is sprouting on Guy the Gorilla's nether regions, then it's time to get to work and harvest the old head crop. I guarantee that it works wonders for the ladies: my own experiences can vouch for that, while Grant Mitchell from *EastEnders* has banged one into the net more times than Bobby Charlton. So if you want to score, it's a case of no more comb-overs and get yourself a crop.

There's another upside to resembling Kojak, as one thing women love even more than running their hands through the contents of a man's wallet is smoothing them tenderly all over a bloke's newly shaved bonce. So voilà, your very own solar-powered love machine!

If, on the other hand, instead of a thinning thatch you resemble some bloke off the telly who paints other people's living rooms hideous shades of purple and pink, wears frilly shirts and talks like he's eating half a ton of marbles, then you'd be better off getting yourself straight off down the local gay club because that's the only place where you'll be getting any attention.

Face

Personally, I have lost count of the number of glossy magazines – and women in salons with faces the colour of the Dutch national strip (that's orange, in case there are any women reading this) – who preach that the only way to achieve great skin is as complex and puzzling as the instructions for a DIY set of wardrobes from the foreign furniture seller in your local retail park.

The simple truth is that your skin is a relatively simple feat of modern engineering and, like your car, will function well enough with only the odd minor breakdown if you maintain it regularly.

Taking care of your skin will not, however, mean spending hours in front of the mirror and it certainly won't turn you into a girl. So you'll still be able to reverse park and there'll be no need to trot off to the gents with half a dozen of your mates in tow either!

The easiest place to start your regime off correctly is with the simple task of washing both morning and night with a mild perfume-free face wash – and, it goes without saying, also straight after you've been elbow deep in your Escort's engine. (Don't use soap, as it'll only dry out your skin and make you smell like the perfume counter at Selfridges.)

Twice a week, scrub your forehead and entire 't' zone with a face scrub, again perfume-free, and leave it on for a couple of minutes as this will loosen any blackheads lurking and also get rid of any dead skin cells, resulting in a face squeakier than Sooty's sidekick. Don't, however, choose one with the consistency of the bottom of your fish tank, as your skin's tough but no Rambo. And after all, you don't want to end up looking like some extra from *Hellraiser*.

Next, I want you to head for the kitchen and boil a kettle. ('Tea?' I hear you ask, 'I thought I was washing?' You are and that kettle holds the key to the next stage to perfect skin.) While you're waiting for it to boil, wash off the scrub, as it's done its job, though be careful not to get any in your eyes otherwise you'll resemble someone who's just taken a gob full of bad beer.

Your skin should be feeling better already, so it's now time to use that kettle. Pour the boiling water into a large bowl then cover your head with a towel and sit with your face over the water for about five minutes while the steam opens your pores. When that's done, rinse your face thoroughly with cool – but not cold – water to temporarily tighten your pores.

Once a week get a face mask sachet from your local supermarket – and don't be embarrassed buying it, as I can guarantee the checkout girls serving you have seen much stranger things on their conveyor belts.

Follow the instructions for use and go and do something else or just relax for the next ten minutes, or for however long it recommends on the packet. Should the doorbell ring in the meantime, either ignore it completely or tell the open-mouthed postman you're busy researching for your up-and-coming role for the film *Braveheart 2*.

When the recommended time's up, rinse it all off again with cool – but not cold – water. It's now time to finish off all that good work. You wouldn't wash your car and not polish it, now would you, and the same applies to your face. Apply a moisturizer all over, avoiding the delicate eye area, and blot the excess with a tissue. You can either buy your own or there's always your mum's 'Oil of Ugly'.

It may sound camper than Dale Winton's shopping list, but don't neglect the skin under your eyes. In a later chapter we'll be discussing your eyes as an important pulling tool, so let's not forget them. They are the first part of your face to droop, so apply a light eye cream on the area between eyebrow and lid and underneath the eye. Be gentle and don't use too much otherwise instead of 'come to bed' peepers you'll end up with ' I need a visit the optician' ones.

Now I know a tan looks good and makes us feel healthy, but go easy on the sun beds. You may think you look better with a slight facial reddening after that alcohol-fuelled two-week 18–30 holiday in Ibiza, but apart from ultimately creating that crocodile handbag look, you're rapidly increasing your chances of contracting skin cancer. So if you must go brown, use a good fake tan or skin bronzer, both of which are available at your local chemist.

We now come to shaving – and I mean you, not her. Believe it or not this repetitive and mundane act is guaranteed to please women. They just adore the feel of a man's smooth chin, as it doesn't tickle their lips when you kiss them and, if you shave without them even having to ask in the first place, then the world is your oyster – they'll see you as sensitive and caring.

The most frequent question at this stage is, 'Which is the right way to do it?' For this, I feel I must blame those men we have looked up to since we could first crawl, notably our fathers. I mean, it's just not fair. Allow me to explain.

As soon as any pubescent female discovers she has

hair growing down below or complains of an upset stomach, her mother whisks her off to the bathroom and teaches her all about puberty, periods and the obligatory talk on where a baby comes from.

Boys, on the other hand, get absolutely no tuition on such matters from their elders. When we find the same curly ones growing wild on our spotty chins, Dad suddenly dons his magic invisible cloak and hides behind his well-thumbed copy of the *Sporting Life* while you – ignorant and bewildered – proceed to hack away at the offending areas with one of Mum's rusty disposables, resulting in a scene that could have come straight out of *Kill Bill*.

Read on and learn how to have a peachy, toilet-paper-free jaw-line.

Firstly I want you to follow the example of your local curry house – and if you're confused, then I'll explain. That lemon-scented hot moist flannel, mistaken by all of us at one time or another for a banana fritter after twelve pints of falling-down-and-giggling water and a chicken madras hotter than Britney's bum, can help you attain your goal. And here's how.

Take a small hand towel, moisten it and place in the microwave for about 30 seconds. (Remember first to remove the remains of last night's baked-on pizza – after all, you don't want a tomato, mozzarella and pepperoni face-mask, now do you?)

Remove it, place it on your beard area letting the resulting steam open your pores. Leave on for a couple of minutes, or until it starts to cool, and then it's time to lather up for the next stage. Rub some shaving gel into your beard area (don't use foam – this doesn't penetrate the bristles enough) and work into a decent lather. This will make the little blighters sit up ready to be lopped off quicker than Henry VIII's exes. Grab hold of a clean double- or triple-bladed turbo GTI-type razor advertised everywhere and shave in the following order:

Start from your sideburn then go diagonally across your cheek to your chin, all the time keeping the skin taut by pulling with your thumb. Continue across the chin and then down the neck, working in the direction of the hair growth. Remember to rinse the blade regularly in clean hot water to remove the shaved hairs and lather.

Never shave against the direction of hair growth, as this may cause irritation (even worse than your old man banging on the toilet door demanding to be let in as he's desperate to use the loo) and possible ingrowing hairs.

Finally, shave your upper lip from the middle outwards, as these hairs tend to be the strongest and should be left till last to allow the lather to fully soften them. After you've finished rinse your face in cool – but not freezing – water, dry and then apply a moisturizing balm or moisturizer to stop the skin drying out. You should now have a smooth, nick-free skin.

Body

This is the bit of you that's usually seen less by a woman than the rest but we're going to try to address this imbalance and get it in tip-top order for when that day finally arrives.

The way to guarantee a body a woman will want to run her hands over is easier than you think and, like the face, starts with the basics of showering or bathing twice daily. Use a body brush or sponge to loosen dead skin cells and make your skin tingle and shine and also remember to condition chest and pubic hair regularly too, as pubes with the consistency of barbed wire will guarantee that the only hand making that southerly journey will be your own.

After drying yourself off, moisturize all over and trim those armpit hairs. You don't have to shave them completely, but women, suckers as they are for cute and furry mammals, won't take kindly to Kevin the Gerbil and Gordon the Gopher being sitting tenants in your underarm department.

Next step is to apply a deodorant. Choose either a spray type or roll-on, although the ball type tends to last longer, keep you drier and women love a man who shows some responsibility for the planet.

You're now done – and you're clean enough to eat off.

Extremities

Your face and hands are seen by others on a daily basis. Your feet are not, so it's time to give them a much-overdue MOT as well.

Let's start with hands, which should be washed regularly and especially after training Terence the trouser terrier at the terracotta. Take special care to clean under your nails as well – if women see that you can't be bothered to clean your nails, there's no imagining what they'll think about the rest of you.

So trim and file the nails regularly, pushing back your cuticles with an orange stick wrapped in cotton wool. Doing this will not elevate you to the Gayboys Hall of Fame – do you really want to be responsible for making her back look like something out of *Nightmare on Elm Street*? I thought not, so start filing or get yourself a manicure. A good hand cream massaged in regularly will also keep them smooth.

Let's now travel downstairs to the feet. In my opinion, feet are just ugly hands and should be treated in exactly the same way, although they spend their time being trodden on and suffocated for most of their lives.

So again, wash them regularly and remember to file the nails smooth as no one wants to be responsible for snagging her Laura Ashley sheets, now do they? Check for any lumps or extra toes growing and should you find any, literally hotfoot it down to your local podiatrist to get them treated. Massage in a good foot cream and that's them finished.

Whether you're happy with the shape of your nose or not, one unwelcome visitor to this body part will cause more damage to your chances of pulling faster than a porcupine in a condom factory, and he is the dreaded dangling nasal hair. It's a mystery to all that after reaching a certain age, the hair on our heads diminishes steadily, whilst the strong, even barb-like thatch that protrudes from our nasal cavities takes on the length and consistency resembling Tarzan's favourite form of jungle transport.

The way to cut its journey short is simple, though many people make the same fatal mistake of plucking. If you do this it'll hurt like hell, you'll cause an infection and end up looking like Rudolph (the reindeer, not the girly tight-wearing Nureyev).

So instead, trim those nasal hairs using sharp nail scissors – taking great care not to cut yourself – and regularly keep an eye on them, as they have a nasty habit of creeping back up on you.

As for the foliage sprouting downstairs, trim it occasionally into whatever style takes your fancy and, apart from cleaning and taking as much exercise as possible (with a partner is better) there's not a lot more you need to do.

Smile

To appear approachable and let someone know that you like them, one of the most important things you can do is smile. Now, if your gnashers can pass for those off the toothpaste ads on telly all well and good, but if they resemble tombstones as opposed to pearly whites then there's no alternative but to make a trip to the dentist for some painful and, dare I say, expensive work on them.

For those of us who find ourselves somewhere in between (and I'm one) here are a few basic rules guaranteed to turn any old common-or-garden frog into a handsome prince.

Start with brushing twice a day, especially after eating, and finishing off with dental floss, but remember to do it gently – you're not sawing wood.

Make sure you visit your dentist at least every six months – and by the way, a 'visit' means actually going in and sitting on the chair, not just popping in to say 'hello' while you chat up the receptionist.

Use a lip balm in winter to prevent chapped lips and keep a breath freshener spray handy. Always check your smile before leaving the house and especially after eating, as the remains of that salad lunch stuck between your teeth looks very much like you've been French-kissing a privet.

It's important too to practise your smile. I know it may sound strange, but you really don't know how you look to others when you're smiling. You may look cool and sophisticated but on the other hand you may resemble one of the competitors off *Come Dancing* – the ones with the fake, Cheshire cat painted-on grins. So practise hard, because flashing just the right amount of enamel may get you noticed, but too much and she could be blinded. Check it and see.

I personally found out about the power of a smile when

I was stripping, as women very often commented on how gorgeous my smile was – which was surprising really, as they had just seen me naked. Women, I ask you ...

Smell

I'm going to let you into a little-known secret about what smells from a man turn a woman on – and believe it or not, it's toothpaste and baby powder.

These two aromas, plus the combination of Mr Bassett's favourite ingredient and something long, green and found in your fridge, are guaranteed to get women swooning.

Women have a much keener sense of smell than men, and therefore the way we whiff can either have them drooling or running screaming for the hills. Obviously, the actual smell matters, but remember, so does the amount – so one other no-no as far as the male musk is concerned is over-indulgence. Go easy because Henry Cooper *was* wrong: splashing it all over just doesn't have the desired effect. Be subtle and don't swim in it.

Too much fragrance can smack of you wanting to cover up some other nasty niff and, even if you are actually lucky enough to get her back to your place, rest assured she'll have passed out long before you've even removed her ear rings, never mind her more interesting bits. And after all, no one likes doing it with a comatose body.

'So, what's the answer then?' I hear you ask, 'what actually works?' Well, what I'm not saying is that you should walk round looking like a cross between Marilyn Manson with a bag of Allsorts and a shuttlecock in your pocket. No, it's much simpler than that. A light dusting with the old white powdery stuff after a bath or shower will make you come across as clean, sensitive and caring – and that means a lot to a woman.

An alternative to talc is a light spray with your favourite aftershave – remembering the rules earlier and not using too much. The ideal way to tell if the particular brand chosen suits you is to spray some on your wrist. If after five minutes you can still smell it, then it's not for you and you should avoid it like the plague.

A cheap and easy way to find out one that suits you is to take advantage of the testers in high-street stores, as while you're at it you can also practise your new-found pulling power on the assistant behind the counter.

Chapter Four | **Dress to impress**

Out with the old ...

Meet the new you

What is the point of following all the good advice given in the previous chapters if you're going to go out beaver-baiting looking like that old dedicated follower of fashion, Mr Jim Royle?

We need only look at our animal cousins to discover what makes us dress up in order to attract a mate. But remember that Mother Nature didn't need an image consultant, and neither do you.

Women, although sometimes simple, are certainly not blind and if you are going to have any luck then you must examine those threads, attack that wardrobe and be prepared to clothe the Third World.

Ninety-three per cent of attraction is physically based. That said, although being able to stand out from the crowd can often be referred to as an art it need not, as is popularly conceived, be expensive. A couple of well-chosen items go a long way to making you look good and, as long as you let the mirror be your guide and not the assistants in the high street, then you're already halfway there.

I'm now going to give you some basic dressing tips that will go a long way to making you look good without you even having to really try. Don't worry if you don't grasp them all at once – we've all of us been fashion victims sometime in our life (me included), so there's no need to worry.

First things first: it's time to attack that wardrobe. Have a good look at what's lurking within and, apart from seasonal coats, clear out and throw away anything that hasn't been worn in the last six months.

Carrying out this one small task will automatically make you feel a hell of a lot better about yourself, as by getting rid of negative items connected with your past you're also ridding yourself of the same negative feelings attached to them. Secondly, you'll now have more room for those new threads you're going to buy on your next trip up west. And thirdly, some toilet-duck-swilling, dog-end-smoking hobo will be kept warm over another bone-freezing British winter courtesy of one of the many charity shops that adorn our high streets. (Apparently, Gucci is popular amongst *Big Issue* sellers I hear.) Carry on like this and soon your wardrobe will contain clothes that you actually want to wear and that you feel good in.

It's now time to hit the shops, remembering to follow some very simple rules:

- When choosing new items, think about what you've already got at home. You want your clothes to co-ordinate so, if shopping for jeans or trousers, wear the shoes and top you're going to be wearing with them. This way it'll look like you've planned what you've got on and not as though you've been dressed by Stevie Wonder in a blackout.

- Try not to buy just one item at a time. Instead, try and get yourself a whole outfit in one go. Women do this best, as I'm sure you'll agree. What bloke can honestly say he has never before in his life heard those immortal words: 'Now I've got those jeans I just must have some shoes to go with them. Oh, and a top.'

Shopping this way means you'll spend a lot less time actually shopping, more time wearing the stuff and all of it will co-ordinate. As time goes on you'll get to know what looks good on you, though remember what suits one person may not suit another, so find your own style and stick to it.

A word of caution here: don't worry about keeping up with the latest fashion. It changes too frequently for most people's pockets and if you do, you'll soon be sending even more stuff to that already overflowing charity shop.

If you don't have one already, then it's time to invest

in the most important piece of furniture to grace your bachelor pad since that La-Z-Boy leather armchair with built in massager and fridge was delivered. 'What is it?' I hear you ask. Well, this must-have item is simply a full-length mirror and it replaces that faithful though flea-bitten mutt as man's best friend, as it doesn't shed hairs, beg for food or leave messy deposits on the carpet. A quick glance in it before leaving the house every day will also let you see how others see you. That way, you can make any desired last-minute alterations before going out and strutting your stuff.

If you've got a body part you're particularly proud of (remember our opening self-confidence chapter), then show it off. That said, don't walk round with your old man flashing and winking his one eye or the only fashion you'll be wearing will be a grey suit with arrows all over it and a number on the chest.

Ignore shop assistants (unless they're gorgeous female ones, then they're fair game) who say you look great in whatever you try on. They often work on a commission basis and will happily divest your wallet of its folding stuff and sell you gear even old orange-haired Happy Meal McDonald wouldn't be seen dead in, so keep them well away from your inside leg.

I'm going to divulge some tips on colour and style

options – first those suitable for skinny sorts and then for those rather more 'generous' takers of Mother Nature's gifts. Make notes on what I've said and next time you're out in the high street you'll get exactly what 'suits you, sir'.

Skinny guys

- Choose horizontal stripes and paler colours to give the illusion of breadth.
- When buying suits, choose loosely cut styles and avoid narrow-cut jackets, which only accentuate your slim frame. Choose a grey background with either large checks or broad stripes to add the illusion of breadth to your physique. Horizontal or diagonal stripes on your tie will also add to that illusion.
- Wear pale trousers to add bulk to your legs, also making sure they are not too slim fitting or too baggy as both draw attention to those pipe cleaners you call your pins.
- Go for bold squares or broad stripes when choosing shirts and add a plain tie or one with horizontal stripes.
- When shopping for jeans, avoid the darker shades and, again, don't go too baggy.
- T-shirts and casual tops should be pale in colour and not too baggy. And skin-tight is a definite no-no.

Short and stocky types

- Wearing darker colours with pale vertical stripes will make you appear taller and leaner.
- Avoid double-breasted suits and go for a soft-cut single-breasted style, making sure the jacket is long enough to cover your bum – otherwise it will look even bigger.
- Choose dark trousers, as they will minimize your bum, and also avoid pleated fronts, as they will make your waist appear larger than it is.
- Make sure your shirt is also dark, but not as dark as your suit, and choose a tie with fine vertical stripes to elongate your body.
- When choosing jeans, make sure the denim is dark and in a fitted style – baggy jeans only increase the bulk of your legs.
- Avoid polo neck tops and instead opt for V-neck styles, again in dark colours, to make your neck appear longer.

I have found personally that the most practical way to choose clothes to suit you is to look around to see what everyone else is wearing. Models in the ads are certainly not representative of normal people, so should not be considered as role models. Let's face it, they're all 25, 8 foot tall, tanned with a six-pack and pecs like Action Man on steroids, with everything they wear looking great on them. So, it stands to reason that you, as a 5' 2" balding bloke with a beer belly and a face the colour of beetroot, will not suit what they're wearing, and vice versa.

If you see a guy in the street who's your height and build and he looks good in his stuff, then make a mental note of what he's wearing and copy him. After all, imitation is the sincerest form of flattery and I think you'll find if you ask him where he got it from he may even tell you.

This worked for me many years ago when I was shopping for new glasses (remember, I was wearing the old wide-screen Joe 90 ones from a young age) and saw a guy wearing a trendy pair of frames. I stopped and politely asked him where he had got them. Not only did he tell me, he actually wrote down the manufacturer, model number and told me how much they were. What a nice bloke.

So, to paraphrase the words of Captain James T Kirk, 'It's now time to boldly go where you've never been before.' Follow these basic rules and that suit you wear to pull in may mean *she* ends up wearing her best suit as far as you're concerned: her birthday suit.

Happy shopping.

Chapter Five | On the pull

The A to Z of
flirting ... Find
your way out of
the maze

'm sorry to have to tell you this, guys, but long gone are the days when you could pull a woman simply by kicking in the door of her cave, wearing nothing but your sabre-tooth double-breasted with pleats and a smile, then dragging her off by her hair back to your bachelor cave for Stegosaurus steaks and some Neanderthal naughties.

Nowadays it's much more difficult than that. The modern independent Miss will have you jumping through more hoops than a dolphin at Sea World before she lets you even get close to her. That said, obviously they're not all made the same and, after studying these mysterious creatures for years, I'm here at last to bring you the practical advice and secrets you need to be transformed into a red-hot woman-winner.

Firstly, we need to look at why women play hard to get, the main reason being that we, the stronger sex (you can tell this book was written by a bloke), let them.

Yes, that's right, us, and it's been like that since time began and Adam gave away one of his ribs (what was he thinking of, fool). Man is a hunter and finds nothing more entertaining than having to fight and chase his prey. So the more they resist the more we enjoy it, although it's not completely one-sided. For while the lion stalks the tasty antelope, imagining how tasty it will be after he's ripped out its throat, the antelope is in turn checking out the lion to see which way it's running and working out its best means of escape using its superior turn of speed.

Relate this to modern times and you will begin to see the similarity. You're in the pub with eyes locked on to your target, the one in the fetching leopardskin top (see, even more similarities). As you prepare to make your move you, like the lion, are also imagining how she will look lying helpless on your Power Rangers duvet (sad). She, in turn, is also checking you out – the way you look, your sense of humour – and working out where the toilets are in case she needs to quickly effect her escape.

It also equates that if you're prepared to put in some solid groundwork in order to pull her, then she'll feel she must be worth the effort and, in her opinion (I know, her opinion doesn't count, but hear me out), you'll have the necessary staying power for the serious relationship she (and all of them) hopes will follow.

So open your eyes and concentrate, for here is the ultimate guide to getting your prey horizontal.

Before we go into detail about actually how to attract a woman, you must first remember that it's not just obvious places like nightclubs and pubs where women congregate. The truth of the matter is that women are everywhere and are all legitimate targets for your pulling skills.

They can be found at work, on the tube, in restaurants, working in shops, dog walking in the park, in the gym – in fact, anywhere. And although we will later concentrate on techniques relating to specific locations, the basics are the same and should be followed and adapted for each situation.

Before you have any hope of getting past first base in the female attraction stakes you must first learn the fundamental (we want fun and they go mental) difference between 'friendly' and 'flirting', as unfortunately most men are hopeless at separating them. This can be seen in practice when an attractive woman talks to a man in, say, a fast food takeaway at the end of a beer-fuelled evening – as, irrespective of the 'friendly only' signs she's giving out, he thinks he's 'in'. Suffice to say that the only thing he's about to receive is the toe of her size-6 stilettos in his groin – and he'll be the one licking his wounds.

A woman, however, is able to separate the two states. She does it all the time and is an expert, so it's up to you to learn the different signs between her being just plain friendly and being interested – as those differences do exist, I promise.

The answer, my friend, is something called body language, and it's the saviour to your dilemma. Body language is the silent way we all communicate with each other, most of time without us even realizing it. As mentioned earlier in the grooming section, only 7% of communication is actually verbal, so that means a hell of a lot of something that is very confusing to us men.

Now, all of us are aware of and recognize the typical everyday signs of body language – such as arms folded, which signifies a barrier. Remember last Friday and the blonde you were talking to for four and a half hours? She was trying to tell you 'I'm cold, tired and bored out of my head and will you please stop looking at my chest!' Another one we are all familiar with is the handshake we all use daily, which translates to us as openness and trust. All of us recognize these and many more physical signs. There are, however, a myriad of subtle signs used between males and females in the body language mating game that need further explanation.

I want you to pay attention and concentrate on what I'm now going to tell you, because I have personally used these techniques and believe me they work. As an example we'll use the scenario of the pub or club – but remember, as I said earlier, these techniques can be used to great effect anywhere. Just tailor them to suit your particular situation.

You should now be well practised with the PSP techniques mentioned in an earlier chapter, so by the time you're in this situation you'll be brimming with confidence and the rest will be a doddle.

To start, as you enter the room, bar, club or wherever you're going, I want you to frame yourself in the doorway for a second or two, which gives every woman in the room time to turn, look and check you out, and you in turn them.

As you enter, stand tall and don't forget to smile. If there's a focal point in the room, such as a bar, then get yourself over to it, walking tall and being aware of who's in the room and where they're standing. Position yourself against the bar so you've a good view of the rest of the room and start to look around very slowly, checking out the talent and making a mental note of where the most attractive women are standing, what they're wearing, who they're with and if they're looking in your direction.

Remember, it takes a woman only ten seconds or so to form a lasting opinion of you, so first impressions really do count. Don't blow it before you've started. Make yours the very best first impression you can.

If any of the women you do fancy catch your eye, then here's what you should do to start the ball rolling. Start by meeting her gaze for about ten seconds and then look around the room again slowly before returning your gaze back to hers.

If she looks away and then returns to look at you then you're over the first hurdle, as it's obvious she's interested. By looking around the room again after the initial eye contact and then returning your gaze to hers, you're delivering a very powerful message to her subconscious telling her that out of all the women in the room it's her that you find the most attractive.

Doing this also gives you valuable time to again check out the rest of the talent in the room, just in case things don't go smoothly with your intended target. Now repeat the previous action by looking away one more time, again returning your gaze to meet hers. If she's still looking she'll be intrigued and just willing you to come over.

One thing you must not do while looking at her, however, is stare. By doing this you'll only serve to unnerve her, as if you resemble Hannibal the Cannibal it'll be a dead cert that you won't find her on the menu tonight, a nice glass of the old red stuff or not.

Again, remember to smile but make sure it's natural

as there's nothing more off-putting to a woman than a man who wears a grin so forced it looks like he's been undergoing a rather painful session of colonic irrigation. Just relax and be yourself. While she's looking at you it's time to bring into play a very powerful weapon from your arsenal (and I don't care if you support United). While she's looking over, lightly pat or scratch a piece of your anatomy that you feel confident with. It could be your biceps, your chest or even that ultra-trendy (well, for the next three days, anyway) hairstyle you've just paid half a month's salary for. Anything, in fact.

Touch or lightly scratch it while still maintaining eye contact, as this sends a powerful message to her subconscious reinforcing your attractiveness and selling yourself further to her. While you're carrying out this action, check out her body language and pay special attention to her feet. If they're pointing in your direction slightly apart, then it's the green light, so floor that throttle. But, should they be pointing toward that man mountain stood across to her right, then it's amber and you have competition.

If she's in the room on her own, then leave it a minute of two before approaching to see if she's waiting for someone to join her. If she is and it's another female, then it's safe to make a move – but continue to act with caution, as her lumberjack of a boyfriend might just be in the gents and will be hitting you with a fist the size of a small car the minute you launch into your well-practised patter.

If, however, she is on her own, one very important piece of advice is to never to go over taking a mate with you for moral support – you may find he'll end up offering you support of a more physical kind when you're repaid with a kick in the groin. This is simply because hunting in man packs of more than one with a single woman as the target is a definite no-no – it's way too intimidating and should be avoided at all cost.

If she is with a friend you may well be better off taking a mate for support. Why? Well, firstly, you'll have to split them both up and women can be harder to separate than a couple of rutting Rottweilers and secondly, having to divide your time between both of them makes it even more difficult to pull, as you can't concentrate on the pretty one.

Have you ever noticed that you very rarely see two attractive women together out on the town? I have a theory about that, and it's this. The attractive one goes out with the plainer one so she looks even better in comparison, and similarly the plain one goes out with the attractive one so she can feed off and pick up any strays that her mate casts aside. This can be used to your advantage, as your mate can distract the ugly sister while you give Cinders your undivided attention.

One guaranteed way to get a head-start in this business is by being introduced to a lady by a friend – this does away with any 'cold calling', as at least you have something in common to help kick-start the conversation from the off. It also allows you to leap-frog to the head of the queue and break one of the cardinal rules of pick-up etiquette: the 'no touching' rule.

The way to use this to your advantage is when someone introduces you to an attractive friend to say 'hello' and shake her hand. I know it might sound old-fashioned, especially in this day and age, but I'm going to let you into a secret, one that's small but so powerful, about how to really shake a woman's hand that will dispense all your doubts.

Before I do, though, firstly let me explain something about the anatomy of a woman so that you can understand how it works. A woman's wrists and the inside of her elbows are crammed to bursting with sensitive nerve endings so, to take advantage of this physiological characteristic, when taking her hand you should keep eye contact with her and then, as you shake, slowly extend your middle finger so it's just lightly touching her wrist, keep it there for a moment and as you withdraw your hand, lightly drag your finger across her wrist down across her palm, ending contact when your middle finger leaves the very tip of hers.

Watch her face and maintain eye contact as you're doing this and I guarantee you'll see a surge of pleasure run straight across it.

This works for the wrist, so let's progress further up the body to the elbow. Using the same process as before, when guiding this newly introduced friend to her seat or another part of the room lightly touch the small of her back with your palm as you lead her to her seat and then, as she sits, gently help lower her down with the lightest of touches just inside her elbow.

To the untrained observer, it may appear the most innocent of touches, but my God it works wonders. I tried these very techniques with a lawyer I met following a show and I can confirm their effectiveness. The organizer of this particular show introduced us and I shook her hand, all the time keeping eye contact and using the 'special shake'. I asked if she would like a drink and then escorted her to her seat, again using the techniques described. Things soon went to plan and her legs went to jelly. That's how powerful these single touches or a combination of two or three can be, so try them for yourself and be amazed by the results.

It's now time to approach her, but first heed this word of warning. Don't just steam in and unleash a corny one-liner that you committed to memory. You know, the one that comes from your mate down the local who reckons it works every time and has them gagging for it (even though you've never actually seen him with a woman).

Chat-up lines simply do not work. The correct way to success is a simple and short opener. After all, you're only trying to break the ice, not sink the *Titanic*!

As you approach your 'target', remember to position yourself at her left-hand side – it's a scientific fact that information absorbed through a woman's left ear is more likely to be retained, as it's that side of the brain which deals with processing emotional stuff and the like. Men, on the other hand, use 99% of their brain to process porn, booze and football and the other 1% to recall what women tell them.

It's funny, but loads of blokes, even in this day and age, are still put off approaching women because they think their initial opening line should be clever, witty, charming or a combination of all three. This is simply not so. Just start off with a simple 'Hi' or 'Hello' and introduce yourself – after all, it's what you say for the rest of the evening that really matters.

Alternatively, you could use an 'open question' as

your initial opening gambit. At this stage, I think I should explain the differences between 'open' and 'closed' questions, why we use one and not the other, and also give you some examples of both.

A closed question, such as the ever-popular 'Do you come here often?', can only really invite a short, sharp response guaranteed to make her resist you more firmly than Manchester United's back four. The replies can range from a polite but stern 'No', which leaves you racking your miniscule brain for your next line after her 'Get lost you socially inept gerbil', or something even stronger, which will see the room go quiet and you beating a hasty retreat to the comparative safety of the gents, muttering, 'Just my luck to choose a lesbian'!

On the other hand, a well-rehearsed open question posed while standing next to her in a busy bar – such as, 'Why do you think it's so busy in here tonight?' – can only invite a more lengthy response, which in turn leads to continued conversation. Using such an opening line means you've broken the tip of the iceberg and it's now time to start chipping away at the polar ice cap underneath bit by bit. And here's how it's done.

Once you've opened the conversation, let her do the talking. After all, a woman's favourite topic of conversation is usually herself and you are going to indulge her by letting her rabbit on and on about nothing in particular for as long as she likes.

While she's doing this, I want you to take note of what she's saying, maintain eye contact at all times and nod in agreement, making positive noises when it's required or when she comes up for air. You could be waiting for ages, but it'll be worth it.

While she's wittering on, don't be tempted to interrupt her and start banging on yourself about how the Arsenal played a blinder on Saturday or describe your entire extensive Star Trek memorabilia collection. That's a mistake so many men have made in the past and have paid dearly for. Your only job for the moment is to watch and listen, as you will need to store the vital information she's sharing to fall back on later.

While she's talking, look to see if you can spot any encouraging body language signals she's giving off that'll give the game away as to how she's feeling. Here are a few for you to commit to memory, though there are many more:

- She touches and plays with her hair. By doing this she's subconsciously saying to you, 'Look at me.'
- She applies her lipstick in your presence. Carrying out this action while you're there is a sure sign that she wants to

make an effort to look her best for you – and also, applying lipstick is a powerful subliminal sexual message.

- She sits on the edge of her seat during the conversation trying to be as close as possible to you.
- When you offer her a drink, instead of wine she chooses something she can swig sexily straight from the bottle.
- She's still talking to you ten minutes after you bought her that first drink.
- She plays with the neck of her bottle in a rhythmical motion.
- During the conversation she says something like 'Your girlfriend would love that', which is a typical female fishing ploy to discover if you already have a lady in your life.
- She spends more than three minutes in the toilets (which is plenty for her to carry out her ablutions), so she must be tarting herself up for you.

On the other hand, however, should she gabble on with her hands in her pockets, disappear to the place where ladies do their 'Noah' impression (two by twos) and return looking no different, then she's none too fussed about you and is probably only chatting because she's feeling lonely as her boyfriend's out of town.

One very important rule is that while she's talking to you, never let your attention falter. Let your concentration waver for a second and she'll be off quicker than Esmeralda when Quasimodo tried to give her a French kiss. (She didn't half get the hump, you know.)

During the conversation, if she starts to ask you questions then you definitely know you're on to a winner. By doing this she's showing you she wants to keep the conversation going and in turn wants to find out more about you. (Just don't make the mistake of telling her how much you earn and that you still live at your mum and dad's, otherwise it'll be curtains for you.)

In response, keep your answers short and in return start to ask what are known in this business as 'probing questions'. These are open questions that invite the listener to part with valuable information for you to use at a later date. At this stage such questions should be along the lines of where she works, what she does there and what type of hobbies she has. By asking these probing questions you're gathering and storing valuable information about her that you will use to good effect later.

As she's baring her life and soul to you, it's now time to start connecting with her subconscious and putting her under your spell. One way to do this is when she's talking about something she seems really passionate about – it could be a film she's seen recently, a sport she likes doing or a forthcoming foreign holiday destination

– to nod and agree with her and tell her that you feel exactly the same way as she does about it. By agreeing with her and appearing to be on her wavelength she'll automatically start warming to you, making it easier to explore her mind – and her body at a later date.

Let me give you a word of warning at this point: when agreeing with her about the subject she's raving on about, never, ever lie. I know it's tempting to say you have been to Jamaica on holiday when in fact the closest you've been is Bournemouth, that you've seen a film with a French title you can't even pronounce or completed a three-minute mile when you couldn't even manage to keep still for the same duration, but it just isn't worth it.

One example I saw of how not to do it occurred when I watched a friend of mine attempting to chat up some woman after I had taken him with me to one of my shows. She was saying how she loved to go and see strippers and how she fantasized over their muscular bodies and erotic dance routines. He fell into the age-old trap and said that he too was a stripper (he wasn't) and was also extremely well-endowed in the downstairs department (this was a lie as well). The long and short of it was that she asked him for a demonstration and, not wanting to back down and lose face, he had the assembled bar in stitches as he fell over his feet while clumsily attempting to remove his trousers.

As you can see, the moral of this story is 'Never lie to impress a woman.' If you're a mechanic, then tell her. You've more chance of getting somewhere by being honest than if you lie and say you're an airline pilot or something equally ludicrous. Plus, she'll respect you more for your honesty.

While she's talking about this thing she's passionate about, she'll automatically put herself in a happy – and therefore more receptive – frame of mind (remember what was said in the chapter on PSP), so she'll be excited and this is when you strike. Though not literally. The golden rule is never to touch a woman unless she touches you first or you've been introduced, as mentioned earlier. We all have our own personal space and don't like others to invade it without being asked, so don't do it.

Ignore this advice at your own peril. If she leans in towards you to say something and you're too far away, then it's time to move in closer. But if people mistake you for Siamese twins, it's time to shift into reverse.

At this stage in the proceedings it's now time to bring into play a very powerful, almost hypnotic technique that was taught to me by a friend who had worked as a male escort for many years. I used it on many occasions myself – and to very good effect, I can tell you.

When she is at the height of her excitement, talking about her favourite subject, you make a gesture. It need only be a very simple one, innocent to anyone else in the room, but believe it or not it will turn out to be very powerful and significant to her and you.

It could be something like adjusting your watch (but not looking at it, or she'll think you're bored), loosening your collar, or something similarly innocuous. While carrying out this 'gesture', concentrate on maintaining eye contact with her. This results in the imprinting of your gesture on her subconscious mind so that she automatically identifies it with pleasure. Should the conversation start to flag at any stage, or you simply want to refer her back to her excited state, you just repeat the gesture while again maintaining eye contact.

By repeating this gesture, she will again return to her previous excited state of mind and will relate your gesture to her pleasurable feelings. While doing this, still maintain a lookout out for her encouraging body language signals.

Another easy way to tell if she's becoming keen on you is to notice if she copies something that you do, which is a technique called 'mirroring' and a sure sign that someone is interested in you. Try it yourself while talking to her. Tilt your head slightly to one side or pick up your glass and take a drink, looking to see if she follows suit. If she does, then it tells you that things are rolling along nicely. Should she happen to touch you at any time during the conversation, then that's also another green light and a further sign that she's warming to you and inviting a return touch of your own – and who can refuse a lady?

If the conversation starts to flag, then repeat the gesture described earlier or throw in a joke, making sure though that the joke has some relevance to the current conversation and is not just a run-of-the-mill smutty one.

I've told you what to say and when to say it but not as yet actually how to say it (and there are different ways, I can tell you). So here goes. You should speak slowly and in a slightly exaggerated manner in order that she has to really concentrate on what you're saying. Talk more quietly than normal (especially if you have a part-time job as the local town crier), then she'll have to lean closer into you, giving you the opportunity to fire off a sure-fire winning statement like the one below that will, I guarantee, impress her no end.

It's a well-known fact that women carry handbags – and how us men manage without them I'll never know, but we just make do with pockets. It's also a fact that women wear perfume and yet another fact that when out for the evening they frequently disappear to the ladies to touch up their make-up and add another copious squirt of eau de yuck or whatever.

They transport all this paraphernalia around in these bags that are bigger than delivery boy's fluorescent satchels, so all you need do is to take a sneaky peek inside to identify which perfume is flavour of the month and use the knowledge to your advantage.

The ideal time to do this is while she's, say, getting a cigarette out, or when she goes to buy a round of beers, but whatever you do don't get caught rummaging through her bag, otherwise the only hands likely to be stripping you will no doubt belong to a member of Her Majesty's Prisons and of the decidedly hairy male gender.

When she returns from wherever she's been, start to talk to her, leaning in close. Then, remark that you love her perfume, identify it by name and say that it's your favourite. She'll be so impressed that you seem to be taking so much notice of her and can recognize her scent that she'll happily stay with you for the rest of the evening.

If she asks you how you know, just reply that a best friend of yours (female, of course) used to wear the same and how you always liked it. But on no account drone on that it was your ex, the scheming bitch, who dumped you after running up that massive credit card bill and who cheated on you with your dad – you know the sort of thing. Also, remember to speak in a slow, controlled, almost hypnotic manner and don't jabber.

So, after all this groundwork you now know more intimate things about her than her gynaecologist, have complimented her that she smells better than that cup of Bovril you so look forward to at half-time, and it's now time to seal the deal with something called 'phonetic ambiguity'.

Phonetic ambiguity is a very powerful conversational technique whereby words that when used on their own sound quite innocent convey a deep hidden sexual meaning to the recipient when they are incorporated as part of a sentence or phrase and emphasized. This is designed to further act on the recipient's subconscious and open her up to you even more. Try the ones listed below and then think up others of your own. The important words to be emphasized are highlighted, to guide you when making up your own sentences and phrases.

Examples:

- I bet you felt **excited** standing at the top of the Eiffel Tower.
- I saw a **wonderful** sight the other day while out driving.

- You make **hard** work sound so easy.

- I'll be **coming** to that stage myself too, soon.

- I got caught in a downpour yesterday and was **dripping wet.**

- **In you** I think I've found someone who feels the same way.

- **I want you** to know I'm with you all the way.

- It's interesting to know how you feel **deep inside.**

- I bet you feel **on top** of the world when you're doing that.

Litter words like these throughout your conversation and you'll soon have her eating out of your hand.

You've now prised out enough of her personal information to steal her identity. She's drooling like a weight watcher in a cake factory. It's now time to ask her out.

Chapter Six | **Asking her out**

What's the worst
that can happen?

One very important point you need to remember when dealing with women is that they absolutely adore a man who appears to be in control. Why else would stunningly beautiful women shack up with ugly politicians, dwarf-like magicians with awful catchphrases or a bloke who spends his waking hours with his hand up a three-foot duck's bottom?

So you've done your groundwork and now it's time to ask for her number and suggest you meet up again to continue the conversation.

Take her number and make sure you write it down. Never, ever, commit it to memory, as if you're anything like me you will be bound to forget it. And one other thing while I'm at it: never enter it into your mobile in front of her, as she's bound to spy the numbers of all the other girls you've been trying to pull.

The sure-fire way to impress her and remember it is to write it down on something important that you're bound not to lose. Nowadays no one carries a pen as it smacks too much of deliberate pre-planning, so ask the barman if you can borrow one, though you won't need to ask for paper as I'm going to divulge a clever trick I've used to my advantage in the past and I'm sure you'll like.

Whip out a ten or twenty pound note from your back pocket and then write her number on it (or get her to do it), saying you have no paper. Then remember to read it back to her to make sure you haven't made any mistakes or if her handwriting's a bit dodgy.

She'll be well impressed by this because it'll appear that her number is doubly important to you and the higher the value of the note, the more important she'll think she is. So don't try and scratch it on a 50 pence piece – it won't work and she'll be well upset. If coins are all you have left after buying her 18 rum 'n' cokes, borrow a fiver off a mate or ask the barman for some paper as well as a pen.

Remember, don't spend the note elsewhere before you take the number down somewhere permanent, otherwise the only number you'll be calling will start with 0898 and will cost you a damn sight more than a twenty.

One more trick you can do to impress her using that note with her number on it (and for this to be successful, it should really be a twenty pound note at least – you'll see why) is to put it in your back pocket and then tell her you can magic it into the till just by concentrating on it.

She'll obviously say that it's impossible or that you're drunk, but I'm going to tell you how it can be done. Firstly, make sure the place is crowded and you have a friend who's in the know standing behind you.

Make the girl concentrate on the till, telling her 'Keep looking at it otherwise the trick won't work', and you do the same, as if willing the note to travel there. While you're doing this, your mate takes the note out of your back pocket and slips round to the opposite side of the bar, buying a drink and thus getting the note into the till.

When he returns unseen, you ask the barman to look in the till to see if the note with her number on is there. Of course it will be, and she'll be amazed. One word of warning, however, when performing this trick: make sure you use a twenty, as anything smaller may well get given out in change to some other bloke and he'll have her number instead of you!

If, when you ask, she gives you her mobile number, you score 6/10. Her home number gets you a 9. But anything that starts with 0898 gets you zilch, as it's bound to be a long-distance and very expensive relationship. If she refuses to give her number out but asks for yours instead, give it to her as you may still be in with a chance – don't take it as an automatic rebuff. By asking for yours she's obviously still not too sure of you and wants to remain in control. That's fair enough as you never know, you may just have impressed her enough to actually get her to make that call. The other reason for doing this is that she may think you're married or shacked up with someone, so she may want to call you to see if someone else answers. They are crafty, these women.

After taking her number tell her you'll call and actually mean what you say. But if you should change your mind later, then don't ignore her or chuck her number away. Do the decent thing and call or text to let her know, and be honest. Woman are resilient creatures and can stand being let down if the bloke's honest, but can't stand liars. And remember, what goes around comes around, so if you have no intention of calling her then don't even think of taking her number.

After this the timing of your first call is crucial. The rule is to never call the same day, or even the next. You want her to want you to call and so build up her anticipation of your next meeting.

The best time to call is two days after your first meeting, and also when you know for sure she'll be alone. Never call her during work hours unless she tells you it's OK, as she won't be in a good position to talk and may even get into trouble. If she doesn't answer when you call and you get her voice mail then don't hang up – instead, leave a message. One girl I met admitted to me later on in the relationship that she didn't answer my first call deliberately as she thought my voice was so nice she wanted it on tape. I told you women were crafty.

Don't jabber on when leaving your message. Make it brief. Firstly, identify yourself – after all, you don't know how many blokes she gave her number out to last night (at least one if that 'twenty in the till' trick goes wrong)!

Finish by asking her to call you, giving her your number and leaving it at that. After all, you've made the first move, kept to your agreement and the ball's now well and truly in her court. One big no-no to remember when making that first call, however, is to avoid having a few beers to steady your nerves and then teaming up with fifteen of your mates, all of you crammed into a phone box, with you slurring your words down the phone. This combination is guaranteed to get your number quickly and effortlessly erased from her phonebook and you from her memory, for good.

If she does answer when you call, then listen first to the tone of her voice when she first realizes it's you to see if she still sounds interested. She may have been pie-eyed when she gave you the number or be married and now have a guilt complex as wide as the tattoos across her hubby's back, so beware.

If she says 'sorry, wrong number', when you know for certain it's her, then she's obviously had time to think. Similarly, if she slams the receiver down before you've finished uttering the first syllable of your name then admit it boy, you've been dumped before you've even been dated, so bow out gracefully.

For this example, though, we'll dwell no more on the negative but on the positive. So she's there when you call, she's pleased to hear it's you and now it's time for the next step: fixing the first date.

Start by asking her what she's been up to since you last met, remembering again to appear interested and to say that you really enjoyed meeting her the other evening. Telephone conversation has both advantages and disadvantages. One advantage is that she can't see if you are still in your pyjamas, but the major disadvantage is that you can't make use of body language, so you must emphasize your voice even more to get the same message across.

Again, litter your conversation with open questions and, after a while, offer to take her out somewhere you know she'll like (you'll know this if you did your homework when you first met her ...) and also have an alternative back-up day and venue in case she can't make the first.

If she gives you a can't-make-it-that-day excuse or similar, don't get angry and start going off on one at her.

Instead, tell her again that you enjoyed meeting her, tell her to take care and take the opportunity to bow out gracefully. While talking, continue to make yourself sound confident and in control. Another advantage of telephone conversation is that she can't see how much you're sweating and nervously wringing your hands.

When you've agreed a time, date and place to meet then again, as you did with her number, write the details down, as you don't want to seem like an amnesiac on acid when you have to ring her back later because you've forgotten.

Read on and discover more ways to help yourself score.

Chapter Seven | **Pulling tools**

Show them you're not a DIY man

For your information, and in case you hadn't noticed, there are male stereotypes galore portrayed on television and in the media. Unfortunately, they are guaranteed to make the average woman excited just by looking at them in (though preferably out of) their uniforms.

They can choose soldiers, macho rough and dirty, and they adore firemen risking life and limb saving damsels and cats in distress. And then there's Mr Clooney, the white-coated medic with his soothing bedside manner and warm, gentle touch.

Women go all gooey at the sight of these guys. But what about someone who's occupation is, say, a dustman or a factory worker? Greasy overalls, dust-encrusted fingers and a ride in a dustcart just don't seem to have the same effect, now do they?

I'm here to tell you not to fret and that there's no need to start hanging around outside burning buildings or donning a white coat and frequenting your local casualty department. There are numerous other props you can use to your advantage.

I'll list just a few to help you start...

Flowers

Extensive research shows that to impress a woman you really need to make her feel special and cherished and the cheapest and most direct way of doing this is to give them flowers. 'But,' you ask 'how do I give flowers to a woman I have never met before?'

The way forward is to arm yourself with some nice blooms from your local florist, with the general rule being that the nicer the blooms given, the better the result. So, a dozen red roses nicely wrapped is a sure-fire winner, but dandelions hastily plucked from your garden or a bunch of wrapperless wilting stems from the local cemetery will only mean another let-down. Buy the best, get them wrapped and remember to pop in a card bearing your first name and mobile number – though get a plain one, such as 'deepest sympathy' means you won't be getting hers.

Start walking down the street carrying your chosen foliage and I guarantee that within minutes some tasty specimen is bound to offer the following comment: 'Ooh, are they for me?' If she's not your type or is with her bloke, then just smile sweetly and say they're for your sick mum and keep on walking. However, if she does take your fancy then smile, reply 'Actually they are', and thrust them into her sweaty but grateful feminine grasp.

You are now left with two choices. You can continue the conversation, again remembering all you've been taught so far, or you can go for the 'mystery' option by walking away and looking back just the once to check her reaction.

She'll either beckon you back immediately or, mark my words, your mobile will soon be ringing.

Kiddies

That's right you bunch of doubters, those noisy little bundles of water, wind and vomit can assist you in winning with women. It's a well-documented fact that most, if not all, women love kids and the sight of one of the snotty-nosed tykes in a pair of faded dungarees hanging on to your hand as you stroll round the local park is guaranteed to make them go all gooey and interested in you.

Just one look at this scenario evokes their deep-down maternal instinct. Carrying that wailing bundle of snot – while wearing your best designer T-shirt – makes you appear sensitive, protective and caring all in one go. Their imagination starts to run riot and very soon you'll find yourself surrounded by hordes of gorgeous females just wanting to take you (and the little bundle) back home.

However, there are a number of very important rules to remember before hoisting that real-life Cabbage Patch doll on to your shoulders and strolling off armed with only a dummy (apart from yourself, that is) and a half-hundredweight of Wet Ones. It's important to choose an absolute angel of a child, as the sight of you shouting full volume at them as they threaten to unleash more water than the Atlantic Ocean on to the shop floor will definitely not endear you to the assembled mass of watching females. They'll just have you down as some bully who can't hold his temper and you'll be right back to square one.

I used this ploy to great advantage myself when asked to babysit my little nephew. We played football in the park, had an ice cream and I was soon fixing up a date with a beautiful redhead who had taken a shine to both of us, and do you know what? I actually enjoyed the babysitting experience.

So, the answer is as simple as a pocket crammed full of dolly mixtures, an armful of tissues and a smile. Pick them up, shove them under your arm and march into the local park or high street and you'll soon have women following you like the kids in the gravy advert on telly. Awwhhh.

No sprog to sit? Don't worry, the next prop could be for you...

Puppies

Go on – admit it, all of us would be liars if we didn't say that we hadn't sat in front of the old goggle box and gone dewy-eyed at the sight of that honey-coloured bundle of fluff as he gets up to all kinds of mischief while wrapped in 27 feet of perforated bum wallpaper. And women are no different. In fact, they're a damn sight worse than we are, so if you find it impossible to prise your sweet-eating, fizzy-drink-guzzling two-year-old nephew from the latest sadistic and violent computer game, then get yourself a puppy.

If you don't currently own one and a phone box makes your tatty apartment look positively spacious, then borrow one or advertise yourself as a dog walker and make some much-needed cash. But remember, if you do buy one for yourself, that they grow and grow – and a puppy is for life, not just for Christmas.

As with the kiddie, a walk in the park with this yappy little chappie is guaranteed to get you a larger following than your local bank cashpoint spewing out freebies, as again you'll come across as sensitive and caring and they will be queuing up to stroke it. Let them start the canine-centred conversation and then it's up to you. Using all the advice given earlier to continue the conversation and then seal the deal.

You may even see a nice lady walking a dog of their own. This gives you the ideal opportunity to speak to her, as you now have something in common.

If you fluff it or don't pluck up the courage the first time, smile and make a note of what day and time it is, which direction she comes from and whether she walks or drives. Next time you see her again, smile and then lead with an open question that's 'doggie based'. Let her take the bait, and it should go swimmingly from then on.

It really is that easy to become a love GOD. All you have to do is reverse the letters round and get a DOG. You'd be barking not to!

Chapter Eight | **Location, Location, Location**

Any time, any place, anywhere

As mentioned previously, pubs, wine bars and nightclubs are certainly not the only territory for you to hunt in. Women are all around us, with some of the most unlikely venues heralding a vast selection of female fruit just ripe for the picking. Listed below are just a few of these types of location, together with specific techniques that can be employed in them to enable you to take advantage of each and every situation.

Cafés and restaurants

Most waitresses and female staff who work in similar establishments are usually experienced and wary of being hit upon by male customers. They can easily defend themselves with the venom of a spitting cobra – or the swift emptying of the contents of a steaming hot coffee pot straight into the unfortunate male's dungaree-clad lap.

The trick in these situations is to employ an altogether different – and for the recipient, novel – approach. One way is, apart from the obligatory 'thank you', not to say anything at all until it's time to pay the bill. Then, when the time comes leave a hefty tip, look her straight in the eyes and say, 'You have gorgeous eyes' and leave. She'll be so shocked by this that she won't have the chance to reply and therefore this compliment, coupled with your controlled exit, will intrigue and leave her looking forward eagerly to your next visit.

Leave it a couple of days till you return, firstly making sure she's on duty. You'll see that she will immediately ignore all the other punters in the place and make a beeline for your table to wait on you hand and foot.

I personally used this technique to great effect in a wine bar in Doncaster (yes, they do have them there) last winter. The waitress, a tall pony-tailed blonde, was working hard while trying to fend off unwelcome advances from a group of Neanderthals sat drinking in the corner.

Now, I know for a fact that women with long hair only put their hair into a pony tail when they haven't the time or the inclination to wash or style it. By doing this they make the best they can out of a bad situation, though they still don't really feel at their best.

I thought I would use this to my advantage so, as I paid for my meal, I left a hefty tip, smiled at her and said, 'You have beautiful hair', smiled again and then left. She looked stunned but as I walked out of the door

I turned back to look and she flashed me a great big smile with that gorgeous mouth of hers.

I was returning to Doncaster to perform in a couple of days, so I popped in for breakfast. She immediately recognized me and came over. We started chatting and the upshot was that I got her number and saw her quite a few times after that.

Try this for yourself and I'm sure you'll be surprised. Choose a body part that she may not feel too good about, steering clear of the obvious ones she's heard more times than Slade's 'Merry Xmas Everybody'.

Don't be like the rest and you're bound to get what the rest aren't getting!

Gymnasiums and health clubs

As a bodybuilder these places rank amongst my personal favourites for pulling women as they are full of flaxen-haired amazons dressed in figure-hugging lycra, all becoming sweaty and tousle-haired in their goal to achieve the perfect body.

A word of warning here though, fellas. There are loads of mistakes to be made in this pulling palace, so tread carefully otherwise you may find yourself massaging more than a bruised ego.

Here are a few dos and don'ts you should take heed of.

Do:

Speak to her at the water fountain while she's taking a well-earned rest, allowing her to take her turn in front of you, of course. Ask her how long she's been training and then remark that she looks like she really knows what she's doing and that it's obviously working.

Take up a position at the treadmill/stepper/cycle next to the one she's using. Most women tend to do quite a lot of cardio so she'll be a captive audience for at least ten minutes, during which you can build up a rapport.

Ask her to explain a piece of equipment you say you haven't used before and you've seen her using, firstly making sure there are no instructors available. She'll fall for the helpless male specimen and you could always suggest working out together in and out of the gym.

Join in on one of the advertised exercise classes. Get chatting during the floor exercises (if you can speak, that is) and then suggest a cool drink at the juice bar.

Don't:

Try and show off by using too much weight. She won't be impressed, and it's her you want to pull, not a muscle. Sweat all over the machine you're using and not wipe it down afterwards. It's impolite gym behaviour and won't endear you to either her or anyone who happens to lie in it.

Talk to her while she's in the middle of exercising. You'll only succeed in irritating the hell out of her. She may even suffer an injury and you will too if you don't duck as she chucks that dumbbell at you.

Dress in skin-tight luminous Lycra covered in so many logos you look like some yob has been let loose on your kecks with a spray can of paint. She wants to see you, not Versace, Reebok and Nike. Make sure the stuff you wear is comfortable and makes the most of your physique, so no tight shorts if your legs resemble Grandad's old pipe cleaners.

Stand in a group with your mates leering and pointing. It may have taken her all of her confidence to join the gym in the first place and your amateur laddish behaviour will only serve to send her for an early bath – and no, they're not mixed.

As a bodybuilder, I was, believe it or not, at a disadvantage when trying to pull women and I had to use my wits and the above techniques even more when trying to pull. Sure I had a great body, but women felt shy about approaching me as they felt overawed and couldn't compete. So, many times they ignored me and went off to talk to the weedy guy.

Do as I did and concentrate on the dos and avoid the don'ts and you'll get somewhere.

It's quicker by train

Train and underground tube compartments, with their hot, sweaty, high-fee-paying, unhappy customers, do not usually encourage thoughts on social intercourse.

A radically different approach will therefore be required if you're to prise that prissy-looking business hussy away from her laptop. In the past I have used various techniques with varying degrees of success, and will now explain the ones that have worked the best for me.

The first is to try to read – without being noticed, of course – what she's typing or the book or newspaper she's reading. Then, when she takes a break, start the conversation flowing with a relevant question about that subject. If she's reading a novel, ask about the author (this information is available on the back cover) and mention that you're thinking of reading it but as yet haven't got very far. Ask how she's *enjoying* it (a phonetic ambiguous phrase) and very soon you'll be chatting like old friends.

If you're travelling by train, the arrival of a drinks trolley will give you the opportunity to refresh not only her thirst but also your next line. Should she not be reading, then there's always the state of the railways to discuss and, with the numerous and lengthy delays that are now the norm, you'll have even more time in which to get acquainted.

If she gets on during your regular journey, then make a mental note of the time and the stop she gets on and off from so, should the opportunity not lend itself that day, you can always try again the same time same place, as it were.

Next time she gets on, try and keep a seat next to you so she can sit down there, hopefully having remembered you from your earlier conversation. It's a known fact that people hate sitting opposite anyone and making eye contact as they feel uncomfortable, so she's more likely to want to sit next to you.

Help with her luggage if she has any, noting any first names on the label as this is always a good ice-breaker (if not back-breaker – as you know, women don't travel light).

If the train's packed, then offer her your seat and go on from there.

Shops and stores

Supermarkets, shops, stores and the like are full to bursting with women who are looking for a man – and not always one in a uniform – to show them where the avocados are.

Different approaches are required for fellow shoppers and staff, but the end results are the same – you get to carry home and enjoy exactly what you've selected.

Checkout girls can normally be spotted filing their nails and gossiping about the latest boy band or soap opera story, bored witless with their repetitive chosen occupation. They are suitably prime targets for even the most amateurish of men on the pull. However, you must choose your shopping carefully. It's not a well-known fact but checkout girls are all highly-trained psychiatrists. I mean it: after years of swiping bar codes they can tell the type of person you are just by examining the contents of your wire basket.

A friend of mine was single and went to his local Tesco one evening. He was just paying for his goods when the checkout girl asked him if he was single. Sensing the possibility of an imminent result he enquired, 'Is it because I'm buying all these ready-made microwave meals for one?' She, however, put on her best Cruella face and cackled, 'No, it's because you're ugly!' So watch what you're putting in your basket.

Clock her name badge, as it will come in useful, and then start the chit-chat, remembering the golden rule of always using open questions. One classic line I always use, and it's never failed me yet, is when she asks you if you need a hand with your packing – you reply, 'I'm fine, thanks, but I could do with some help paying', as this always gets checkout girls smiling and you can continue on from there. However, keep your chat short as you don't want a queue forming and risk the checkout girl getting a telling off from the supervisor – or you one from the white-haired old granny who's been waiting ages just to buy a tin of cat food.

When it's time to pay there's another fantastic tip to test the level of her attraction (apart from her eyes, of course – if she looks directly at you when giving you your change, then she's interested) and that is to note how she hands it to you. In this day and age plastic is all the rage, though you're better off always dealing in hard cash in the supermarket. Why? Well, if she puts your change on the counter for you to pick up then she herself doesn't want picking up, it's that simple. If, however, she gives you your coins and lingers flesh on flesh, maintaining eye contact, then there's a good chance she's interested.

Leave and take your purchases with you, remembering to smile and make a mental note of the time and day. Checkout girls usually work to regular shift patterns, so it's odds on she'll be there again, same time next week, for you to work more of your magic on.

When you go back, get her to serve you again. You can always utilize the technique detailed in the 'On the pull' chapter of this book by standing and surveying the lines of tills and, when she looks up and sees you, walking over and depositing your goods on her conveyor belt.

It'll have the same effect on her, as she'll be impressed you've chosen her over all the rest. Work your magic on her further and I guarantee that by the third visit (you should ask her out on this one, otherwise she may lose interest) she'll look forward to you coming.

So those are a few techniques to pull checkout girls. Now we'll concentrate on fellow shoppers. One way to attract them is to take advantage of, and play on, the maternal instinct they all possess naturally. The way to do this is to make your way over to the deli counter and ask the beauty in the queue if she can possibly tell you how to prepare the strange-shaped vegetables you've put in your basket.

Tell her you're not really a naked chef but could be tempted, and as women have a failing for the butter-wouldn't-melt, little-boy-lost look, she will be only too happy to spend some time with you and explain how to boil your shallots. In return, offer to treat her to a coffee in the in-store cafeteria so she can impart more of her culinary expertise and you can get to know her better.

Alternatively, lightly bump trolleys with her, smile, apologize and insist you exchange personal details for insurance purposes as you may well want to sue for whiplash. This one always gets a giggle and you can then offer to help with her shopping as even in this day and age women still love a gentleman.

So there you have it, a few specific pick-up tricks that can be applied to many different venues.

Chapter Nine | **The first date**

Now's your chance – don't blow it

Before the actual date you will need to step up your grooming regime and then plan exactly what you're going to wear. I don't need to tell you that jeans to the opera and a tuxedo to the pub are likely to raise an eyebrow, so choose carefully.

You've used all the information gathered like a hibernating hamster at the first meeting and have arranged to meet at a location you know she'll like, so that's one less thing you've now got to think about.

As far as the actual date is concerned, one no-no to remember is turning up late – as is coming too early.

Keeping her waiting for 20 minutes will either result in her impersonating the invisible woman or, if she is actually still there when you arrive sweating and panting, she'll be at best thoroughly upset and at worse spitting feathers. So, if at all possible, park somewhere close where you can see her arrive, then stroll up nonchalantly looking surprised and comment on the apparent coincidence.

One thing I've forgotten to mention, and a practical

piece of pre-date advice that I've used myself, is to ask a friend to call you on your mobile at a pre-arranged time, say an hour after you meet her. Make it later if you're going to the cinema, as the shrill ringing of 'Greensleeves' while Patrick Swayze walks off into heaven leaving doe-eyed Demi blubbing may well be met with raised voices and a barrage of toffee-flavoured popcorn and strategically aimed strawberry bonbons.

This way, if in the cold light of day, you decide you don't really fancy her, you can make your excuses and leave. However, if you do like the look of her, then answer it and tell your mate not to wait up.

During the first part of the date, again remember the rules of conversation, but this time you can relax a little as a lot of the groundwork has already been covered.

If you've been to see a film, then take her for a drink afterwards to discuss it and carry on the conversation again, making note of her reactions to your open questions and her body language. A lot of people think that the cinema is as unsuitable a date as a brewery is for a meeting of the AA – after all, it's not exactly a place where conversation is encouraged. This is so, but it also gives you oodles of opportunity to check her out without her noticing and the chance to enjoy close physical proximity without the need for an excuse.

The film's finished and you're both sat in the pub, getting on like the proverbial house on fire. Avoid taking her to the sort of places you usually go to, as she won't want to meet your mates this early in your 'relationship', and certainly won't want to be confronted by your ex of two weeks' standing, spitting venom like some hooded she-cobra.

Offer to pay for everything, but if she insists on paying her share then let her, as the last thing you want is to come across as bossy and domineering. By now you're at that stage where the formalities have long since been dispensed with and it's time to make her feel that you've known each other for a long while, not just met. Any woman is far more likely to sleep with someone she feels she already knows as opposed to a total stranger.

The technique I'm now going to explain is called 'emotional bonding' and has the powerful effect of putting her in a higher emotional – and therefore even more receptive – state of mind than normal, one which is more open to your suggestions.

It's a little like hypnosis. You should start to use certain phrases in your conversation, similar to the ones detailed in the 'On the pull' chapter, that have the effect of playing on her subconscious. These can be as simple as saying you loved the film you just watched together, eating the same foods or using more specific phrases such as:

- I **feel** exactly the same way as you do.
- Isn't that an **amazing** coincidence?
- I've always **felt** like that.
- I've always **felt** like that and thought I was the only one.

When she's reached this emotional 'high' again, it's time to push further in search of your goal. Ignore the advice given earlier when I said to let her lead on the conversation. Instead, it's time for you to take the lead, and as you do, gradually litter your sentences with further subliminal messages and powerful verbal commands such as:

- Want it
- Do it
- Take it
- Need it
- Use it

Make sure that while using these words you do not deliver them in a prominent sexual context, as this is her job. You deliver the messages in a seemingly innocent way and it's up to her subconscious to turn them around to convey a deep sexual meaning.

So do not mention sex at all. Instead, let her imagine it through her subconscious being bombarded with phonetic ambiguities and it'll soon be her suggesting it – and that's a promise. As the date continues, try using rather more powerfully sexually suggestive phrases to make her succumb to you even more quickly, such as:

- Surrender
- Open
- Penetrate
- Come over

Remember not to overemphasize these phrases too much. Instead, let her mind do the work. After all this you're now ready for stage two. Instead of just mentioning single words within sentences or phrases, I want you to slowly turn up the pressure and heat by describing an actual pleasurable physical action, which will have the effect of heightening your date's mental state even further.

You should still have the information to hand from your initial meeting, so choose something she mentioned that she really adored. If she mentioned a particularly enjoyable holiday location, then start to describe lying on a white sandy beach, the sun hot over her body, the turquoise water gently lapping her feet, then progress further by describing firm hands massaging sun cream into her bare flesh.

If she mentioned previously that she just adores Belgian chocolates, then start by talking her through choosing one, the shape, the texture and progress to her tasting it, her tongue feeling its coolness and then biting into it, feeling it creamy and delicious on her tongue and throat.

Ask her to imagine such a scenario and instead of you describing it, ask her to describe it to you herself. As she does so you'll immediately notice her face flush with excitement, her eyes widen and she'll be in such a highly-charged state, sexually and emotionally, that she'll soon be putty in your hands.

It's now time to strike and suggest a nightcap back at either hers or yours and get ready for the fireworks. If she still isn't ready to succumb, then don't despair, as Rome wasn't built in a day (Telford was, though). If you've got this far without an imprint of her palm across your gob, then you've obviously made a favourable impression and, with a little more work, you're bound to get there in the end.

It's now time to walk or drive her home and seal all that hard work with a kiss, though it's amazing how many guys do everything right up to this stage and then spoil it all by sucking the lady's face off like wet haddock.

There are more pitfalls in the old kissing game than in a Welsh miner's photo album, so listen on and you'll be guaranteed not to trip up. The most important piece of advice is to let yourself be led by the lady during the act of kissing, as people generally like to kiss someone in exactly the same way they like to be kissed themselves. So don't be a bull at a gate. Instead, let her take the lead and then follow what she does. Notice where she puts her hands, the strength of her kisses. Does she use her tongue? And how passionate is she?

The best type of practice for kissing is to do it as much as possible, so make a second date and remember that even the pied piper started with just one rat following him. Before you know it you'll have her and even more like her following you, so may I wish you the best of luck.

Epilogue | **Author's comments**
So good you won't
tell your mates

I hope you've enjoyed reading this book and have learnt a lot from it. The path to great seduction is full of pitfalls, but I hope that you are now better equipped so you can go out and start living life to the full.

Remember, this stuff is not made up. I personally used all of the techniques mentioned and was transformed from a geek to a god. It certainly worked for me and I guarantee it will work for you.

The best of luck.

RS Webb